Smithsonian

Earth and Beyond

Silver Dolphin

Silver Dolphin Books
An imprint of Printers Row Publishing Group
A division of Readerlink Distribution Services, LLC
10350 Barnes Canyon Road, Suite 100, San Diego, CA 92121
www.silverdolphinbooks.com

ISBN: 978-1-68412-657-6
Manufactured, printed, and assembled in Dongguan, China.
RRD/04/19
23 22 21 20 19   1 2 3 4 5

Amazing Earth written by Courtney Acampora
Animal Habitats written by Kaitlyn DiPerna
Natural Disasters written by Emily Rose Oachs
Outer Space written by Ruth Strother

Amazing Earth, Animal Habitats, and *Natural Disasters* reviewed by Dr. Don E. Wilson, Curator Emeritus of the Department of Vertebrate Zoology, National Museum of History, Smithsonian.

Outer Space reviewed by Andrew K. Johnston, Geographer for the Center for Earth and Planetary Studies, National Air and Space Museum, Smithsonian.

For Smithsonian Enterprises:
Kealy Gordon, Product Development Manager, Licensing
Ellen Nanney, Licensing Manager
Brigid Ferraro, Vice President, Education and Consumer Products
Carol LeBlanc, Senior Vice President, Education and Consumer Products

Image Credits: Thinkstock, Getty Images, NASA

CONTENTS

A NOTE TO PARENTS AND TEACHERS

Smithsonian Readers were created for children who are just starting on the amazing road to reading. These engaging books support the acquisition of reading skills, encourage children to learn about the world around them, and help to foster a lifelong love of books. These high-interest informational texts contain fascinating, real-world content designed to appeal to beginning readers. This early access to high-quality books provides an essential reading foundation that students will rely on throughout their school career.

The five levels in the Smithsonian Readers series target different stages of learning abilities. Each child is unique; age or grade level does not determine a particular reading level.

When sharing a book with beginning readers, read in short stretches, pausing often to talk about the pictures. Have younger children turn the pages and point to the pictures and familiar words. And be sure to reread favorite parts. As children become more independent readers, encourage them to share the ideas they are reading about and to discuss ideas and questions they have. Learning practice can be further extended with the quizzes after each title.

There is no right or wrong way to share books with children. You are setting a pattern of enjoying and exploring books that will set a literacy foundation for their entire school career. Find time to read with your child, and pass on the amazing world of literacy.

Adria F. Klein, Ph.D.
Professor Emeritus
California State University San Bernardino

Amazing Earth

Courtney Acampora

Contents

Amazing Earth

Earth is an amazing planet.

Earth is made up of seven **continents**.
Each continent is **unique**.

North America

North America is a continent.

It includes the United States, Canada, and Mexico.

Canada

United States

Mexico

North America has mountains. It has deserts and beaches.

The Grand Canyon

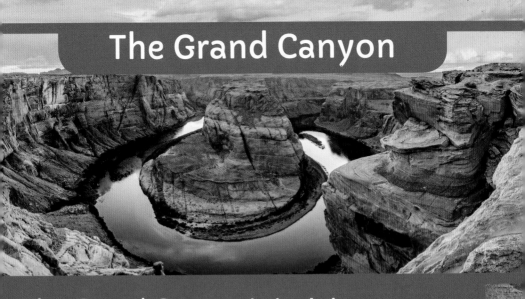

The Grand Canyon is in Arizona.
It was formed by the Colorado River.
It is millions of years old.

The Grand Canyon has amazing sights.

North America

Denali

Denali is in Alaska.

It is the highest mountain in North America.
Denali was called "Mount McKinley" until 2015.

Carlsbad Caverns

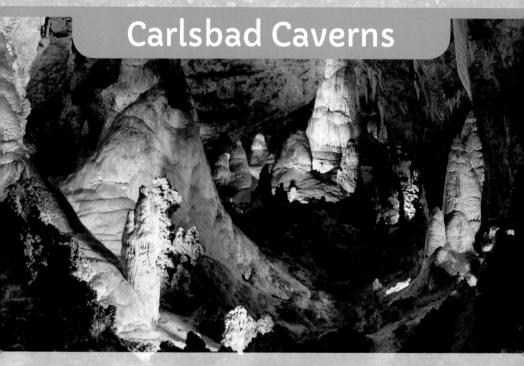

The Carlsbad Caverns are caves.
They are underground in New Mexico.
They were created millions of years ago.
The caves were once part of an ocean!

South America

South America is a
large continent.
It is connected to
North America.

South America has rain forests.
South America has many interesting
cultures.

Angel Falls

Angel Falls is in Venezuela.
It is the highest waterfall in the world.
It was named after Jimmie Angel.
Jimmie Angel was an American aviator.
He saw the waterfall from a plane in 1933.

South America

The Amazon Rain Forest

The Amazon is a giant rain forest.
It is a **habitat** full of plants and animals.
It has more wildlife than anywhere else
on Earth.

Atacama Desert

The Atacama Desert is in Chile.
It looks similar to the planet Mars.
New space **technology** is tested there.

Europe

Europe has forty-four countries.
Europe has many manmade landmarks.

It has many landscapes such as mountains, beaches, and **tundra**.

Reindeer Migration

Thousands of reindeer **migrate** from Norway to Finland.
They travel across the ice.
They feed on grasses in the summer.
The reindeer travel to a new home each winter.

Europe

White Cliffs of Dover

The White Cliffs are in England.
They are white from seashells and sea creatures.
They were formed millions of years ago.
The cliffs are ten miles long.

Iceland is home to fire and ice. Iceland has one hundred and thirty active and inactive volcanoes.

In 2010, a big volcano erupted in Iceland.

It is also home to the largest **glacier** in Europe.

Africa

Africa is a large continent.

The Sahara Desert is in the north.
The Nile River is located in Africa.
Many animals live in Africa.

Massive Migration

The Serengeti is a savanna.
A savanna is a grassland.

Wildebeest, zebras, and gazelles migrate
in the savanna.
They head north in the spring.
They head south in the fall.

The Nile River

Mediterranean Sea

LIBYA

Alexandria

Damietta
Port Said

ISRAEL

SYRIA

JORDAN

CAIRO
Giza

Suez

SINAI

SAUDI
ARABIA

Siwa

Bahariya

EGYPT

Sharm el-Sheikh

Farafra

Kharga

Nile

Luxor

Red
Sea

Dakhla

Aswan

Lake
Nasser

SUDAN

The Nile is the longest river on Earth.
It is located in Egypt.
The Nile River is an important source
of water.

Mount Kilimanjaro

Mount Kilimanjaro is a large mountain.
It is known as the "Roof of Africa."
The mountain is made of volcanoes.
It was formed around a million years ago.

Asia

Asia is the largest continent in the world.

Asia has deserts, tundra, and tropical beaches.
It is also home to two-thirds of the people on Earth.

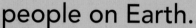

Mount Everest

Mount Everest is the tallest mountain above sea level.

It is in the Himalayas.

It slowly grows taller each year.

The Dead Sea

The Dead Sea is in the Middle East.
The Dead Sea isn't a sea.
It is a lake.
The Dead Sea is full of salt.
Plants and animals can't live in such salty water.

Gobi Desert

The Gobi Desert is a cold desert.
It is located in central Asia.
It can be minus forty degrees
Fahrenheit.
The Gobi Desert is mostly rock.

Antarctica

Antarctica is at the bottom of the planet.

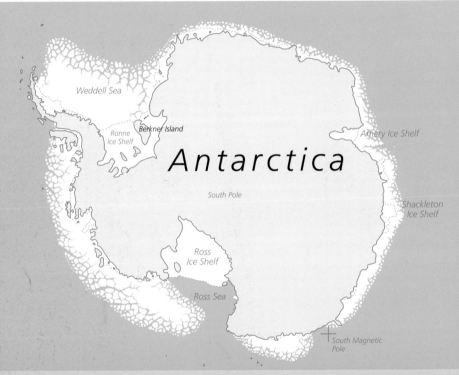

Weddell Sea

Ronne
Ice Shelf

Berkner Island

Amery Ice Shelf

Antarctica

South Pole

Shackleton
Ice Shelf

Ross
Ice Shelf

Ross Sea

South Magnetic
Pole

It is cold and icy there.
Antarctica is always covered by a
thick layer of ice.
The ice never melts completely.

Australia

Australia is the smallest continent.
Australia is a continent and a country.
Australia has many unique animals.
They are found nowhere else in the world.

The Great Barrier Reef

The Great Barrier Reef is a large coral reef.
It is the largest living structure in the world.
It can be seen from space.
It is home to twenty-five percent of ocean life on earth.

Australia

The Outback

The Outback is a large, dry region.
It takes up most of Australia.
Uluru (Ayers Rock) is in the Outback.
It is a giant sandstone.

NEXT
20 km

Earth is home to many unique sites.
Earth has volcanoes, coral reefs, and
much more.
Earth is an amazing planet!

Amazing Earth QUIZ

1. How many continents does Earth have?
   a) Five
   b) Ten
   c) Seven

2. What formed the Grand Canyon?
   a) An earthquake
   b) The Colorado River
   c) The Pacific Ocean

3. Why are the White Cliffs at Dover white?
   a) From volcanic ash
   b) From seashells and sea creatures
   c) From quartz, a type of rock

4. What is the tallest mountain above sea level on Earth?
   a) Mount Everest
   b) Denali
   c) Mount Kilimanjaro

5. Which continent is the largest?
   a) Asia
   b) North America
   c) Africa

6. What is so big it can be seen from space?
   a) The Outback
   b) The Amazon Rain Forest
   c) The Great Barrier Reef

Answers: 1) c 2) b 3) b 4) a 5) a 6) c

GLOSSARY

Continents: seven large landmasses on Earth

Culture: customs and beliefs of a group of people

Glacier: a large mass of slow-moving ice

Habitat: place where plants and animals live

 **Migrate:** move from one habitat to another

Technology: machines and equipment developed to solve problems

Tundra: Arctic region with  frozen soil and no trees

Unique: the one and only of its kind

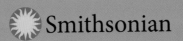

Animal Habitats

Kaitlyn DiPerna

Contents

What is a Habitat?

The natural home of an animal is called a **habitat**.

Different animals live in different habitats.

A whale's habitat is the open ocean.

A polar bear's habitat is the Arctic.

A lion's habitat is the savanna.

Welcome to the Jungle

More than half of all the animals on Earth live in the rain forest.

Rain forests are warm and rainy.
Rain forests have lots of tall trees.

Brightly colored parrots fly through the rain forest.

Monkeys swing on jungle branches.

Jungle leopards' spots help them hide in the shadows.

Wide Open Savannas

Savannas are wide-open spaces with tall grasses.

Savannas are hot and dry.

Savannas do not get much rain.

When it does rain, grass grows and animals have water to drink.

Lions hunt in the tall grasses.

Elephants play in the water.
Giraffes eat leaves from tall trees.

Zebras gather in **herds**. Their stripes help them to blend together.

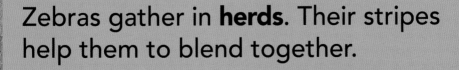

Extreme Deserts

Deserts are very dry places.
Some deserts do not have any rain for years!

Deserts can be very hot during the day.
Deserts can be very cold at night.

Camels can survive without water for days.

Owls hunt at night, when it is cooler.

Rattlesnakes hide in the shade of rocks and plants.

At night, coyotes call to each other across the desert: "Owoooah!"

Earth's Forests

Forests have cold winters and warm summers.

Some forest animals survive by **hibernating** in the winter.

They go into a deep sleep for months!

Foxes use their bushy tails as a warm cover in the cold.

Grizzly bears stand in streams to catch their favorite meal: salmon.

Porcupines have sharp quills for protection.

Male deer grow antlers in the summer.

The antlers fall off in the winter!

Mountain Life

Mountains have high winds, ice, and snow.
Mountains are rocky and rugged.

Animals that live in the mountains have to be good climbers.
Mountain goats have hooves that can grip the rocky ground.

Groups of llamas live together in herds on mountainsides.

Chinchillas have soft, thick fur to keep them warm.

Mountain lions are **predators**. They hunt other animals for food.

The Icy Polar Regions

The South and North Poles are extremely cold.

Ice covers the poles year-round.

Arctic animals have special features to protect them against the cold.

Penguins' feathers are waterproof to keep them dry when they swim to find fish. When the penguins are on land, they huddle together in groups to keep warm.

Polar bears' cream-colored coats help to hide them against the snowy landscape.

Walruses and leopard seals come onto the ice to rest.

Unique Islands

An island is a small piece of land surrounded by water.

Islands can be home to **unique** animals that can't be found anywhere else.

More than one hundred different types of lemurs live on the island of Madagascar.

Kiwi birds are native to New Zealand.

These small birds cannot fly.

Flying foxes aren't foxes at all. They are bats that eat fruit!

Galápagos giant tortoises live to be over one hundred years old!

Komodo dragons are huge lizards that can grow to be ten feet long!

They eat nearly anything, including pigs, goats, and even other Komodo dragons.

Freshwater: Lakes, Rivers, and Ponds

Only three percent of the water on Earth is fresh water.

Fresh water can be found in tiny puddles or great lakes, in small streams and mighty rivers.

Many fish that live in rivers have to be strong swimmers so they don't get pulled by the **current**.

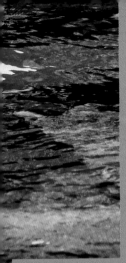

Salmon live in the ocean but they swim up rivers to where they were born.

Canada geese **migrate** when winter is coming.

They fly long distances to warmer weather.

Beavers use their strong teeth to cut down small trees and branches.

They use the branches to build dams.

Wetlands and Swamps

Wetlands and swamps are areas with shallow water and grasses.

Wetlands and swamps may be freshwater or saltwater, like the ocean.

The Everglades is a flooded wetland and a national park.

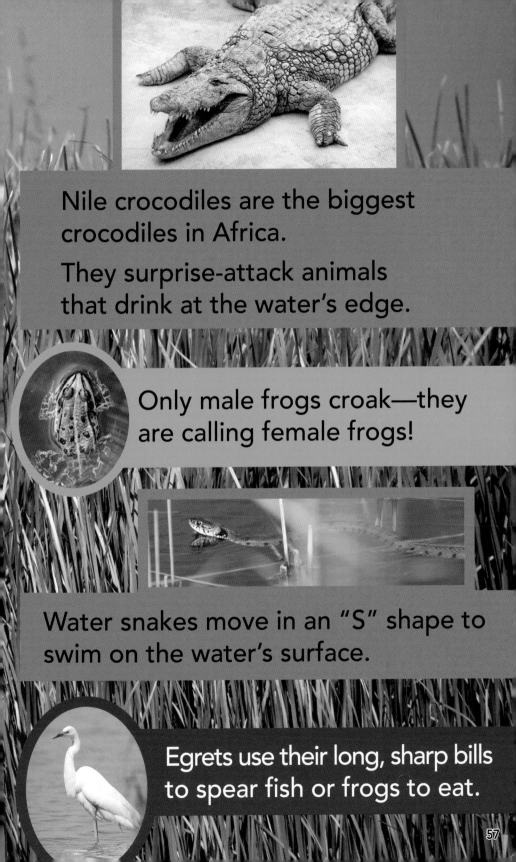

Nile crocodiles are the biggest crocodiles in Africa.

They surprise-attack animals that drink at the water's edge.

Only male frogs croak—they are calling female frogs!

Water snakes move in an "S" shape to swim on the water's surface.

Egrets use their long, sharp bills to spear fish or frogs to eat.

Coastal Waters and Tide Pools

Coastal waters are the shallow parts of the ocean by the shore.

Tide pools are rocky pools by the shore that fill with water.

The tide affects coastal waters and tide pools.

The tide causes the ocean to rise and fall twice each day.

Manatees and dugongs are gentle giants that live in warm coastal waters.

They are mammals, so they need to come to the water's surface to breathe.

Sea otters float on their backs.
They hold onto kelp so they don't float away.

Most sea stars have five arms, but some have ten, twenty, or even forty arms!

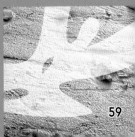

Colorful Coral Reefs

Coral reefs are made from tiny animals called polyps.

The polyps have a hard shell like a snail.

The polyps join together and their shells make a reef.

Coral reefs are home to more types of fish than anywhere else in the ocean.

Reef sharks have sharp, triangular teeth.

Sea turtles feed at coral reefs.

Sea turtles only go on land to lay eggs.

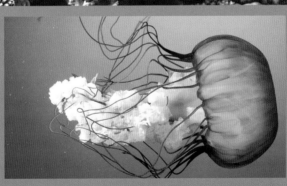

Jellyfish are not fish, but they do feel like jelly!

But don't try to touch them—some sting!

The Open Ocean

The ocean covers more than seventy percent of Earth's surface.

The open ocean has warm tropical waters, and cold icy waters.

Many ocean animals migrate long distances in the ocean to find food.

Blue whales are the largest animals on the planet.

The heart of a blue whale can weigh as much as a car!

Dolphins travel in groups called pods.

They talk to each other with whistles and squeaks.

Flying fish can swim fast enough to break the water's surface and glide through the air!

Protecting Animal Habitats

Animals are only able to live in certain habitats.

Some habitats are disappearing.

Forests are being cut down.

Polar ice is melting.

It is important to protect animal habitats. We can protect habitats by recycling, using cars less, and not **polluting**.

We want all the animals on Earth to have a home!

Animal Habitats QUIZ

1. Which habitat does a lion live in?
   a) Savanna
   b) Desert
   c) Rain forest

2. Which habitat is home to more than half of the animals on Earth?
   a) Rain forest
   b) Freshwater
   c) Desert

3. What does hibernating mean?
   a) Hunting for food
   b) Finding a mate
   c) Going into a deep sleep

4. Where are kiwi birds from?

    a) Africa

    b) New Zealand

    c) Madagascar

5. What are coral reefs made from?

    a) Algae

    b) Polyps

    c) Krill

6. The ocean covers how much of Earth's surface?

    a) Seven percent

    b) Seventy percent

    c) Fifty percent

Answers: 1) a 2) a 3) c 4) b 5) b 6) b

GLOSSARY

current: water moving in a certain direction

habitat: place where an animal lives

herds: large groups of hoofed animals

hibernating: going into a deep sleep during the winter

migrate: to move from one area to another for feeding or breeding

polluting: spoiling something with trash and waste

predators: animals that hunt and eat other animals for food

unique: unlike anything else

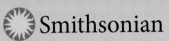
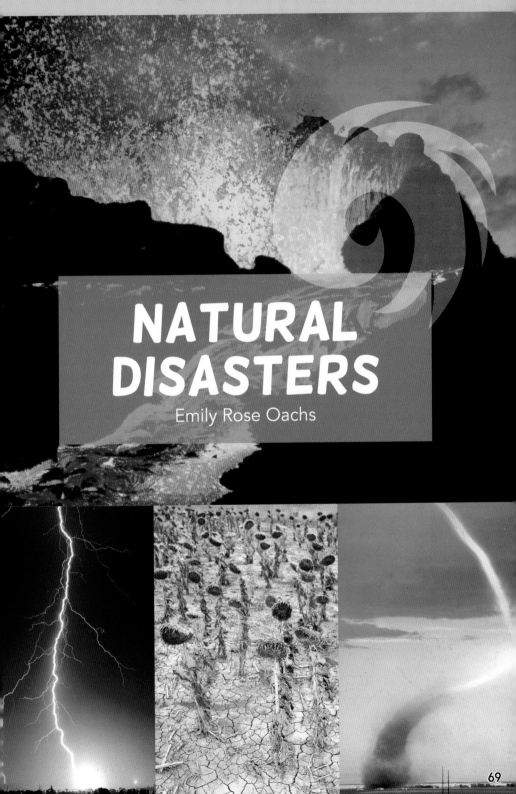

NATURAL DISASTERS

Emily Rose Oachs

CONTENTS

WHAT IS A
NATURAL DISASTER?

Natural disasters happen naturally on Earth.

Natural disasters can cause a lot of damage.

They can put lives in danger and even change Earth's landscape!

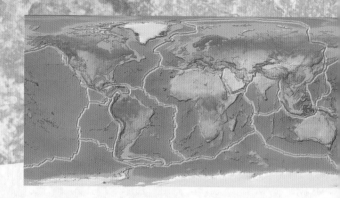

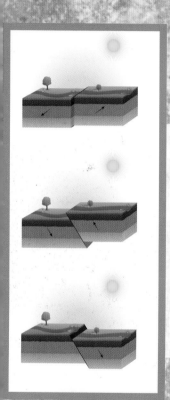

Big slabs of rock called **tectonic plates** cover Earth.

When tectonic plates move they cause the earth to shake.
They cause earthquakes.

Earthquakes feel stronger the closer you are to their **epicenters**.

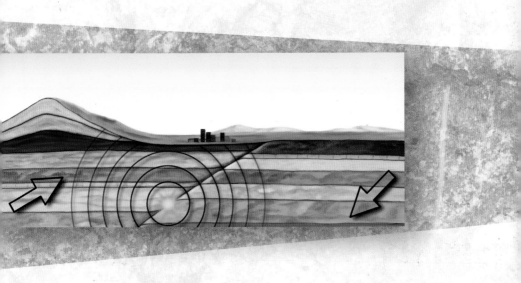

Large earthquakes can be felt hundreds of miles away from their epicenters!

A tsunami is a series of big waves, called a wave train.

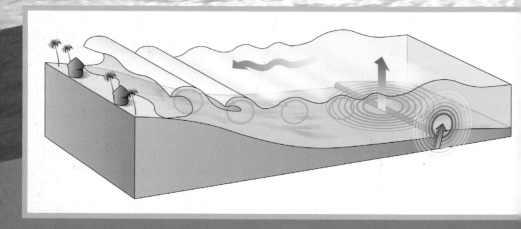

A tsunami can be caused by earthquakes, volcanoes, or landslides.

Tsunami waves speed through deep ocean water.

On the coast, they sweep away buildings, trees, and anything else in their path.

A volcano is a vent in the Earth's crust that erupts.

Ash, lava, and gases come out of the volcano.

The **mantle** is beneath the Earth's crust.

The mantle is so hot it melts rock.

Melted rock comes out of a volcano as lava.

THUNDERSTORMS

Thunderstorms are rainstorms with thunder and lightning.

Thunderstorms form when warm, moist air rises in the **atmosphere**.

As the air rises it cools and forms fluffy thunderclouds.

Ice and water droplets collide, creating electricity.

Lightning bolts form to get rid of the electricity's energy.

The heat from the lightning causes the air around it to vibrate.

Thunder's noise comes from the vibration.

A tornado is a violent windstorm with a spinning, funnel-shaped cloud.

All tornadoes come from thunderstorms.

Tornadoes have the fastest winds on Earth.

Their winds cause a great deal of damage.

HURRICANES

Hurricanes are massive, swirling tropical storms.

They bring strong winds, heavy rain, and tall waves.

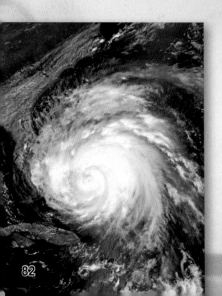

Most hurricanes occur in late summer and early fall.

Hurricanes form above warm, tropical water.

They can grow up to almost 600 miles across!

FLOODS

Floods are common weather-related disasters.

They occur when heavy rain falls for a long period of time.

Heavy, moving water can be destructive.

Floodwaters wash away buildings, roads, bridges, and people.

DROUGHTS

Droughts occur in areas that receive less rain and snow than normal for a long time.

Water is an important part of life.

Humans, animals, and plants need water.

But during droughts, water is scarce.

During droughts, the ground becomes dusty and cracked.

Wildfires become more likely during droughts.

Wildfires are uncontrollable fires that spread quickly.

Wildfires occur in dry, hot seasons.

Dry areas are more likely to catch fires.

Dry plants are fuel for flames.

Strong winds spread the flames.

Firefighters attack wildfires with water.

Avalanches occur when large amounts of snow and ice flow down a mountain slope.

Avalanches begin when snow breaks free from a mountain.

As it moves, it picks up speed and more snow, ice, and rocks.

Avalanches slide with deadly force.

They wipe out villages in their paths.

MUDSLIDES

A mudslide is a disaster when masses of soft, wet land flow down a slope.

A mudslide can travel miles.

Mudslides occur in areas with heavy rainfall

The ground becomes so wet it can't receive any more water.

This makes the ground soft and unstable.

Mudslides move fast and sweep up everything in their path.

EPIDEMICS AND PANDEMICS

An epidemic is a widespread outbreak of a disease or illness.

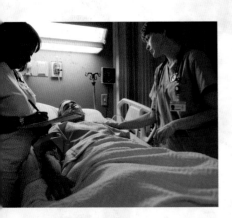

Thousands of people can become ill in a short amount of time.

How people become infected depends on the disease.

When an epidemic spreads outside a community it becomes a pandemic.

Pandemics spread across a wide area, or even the world.

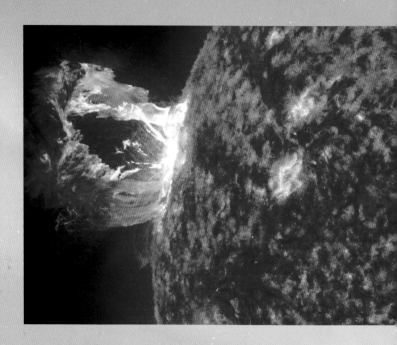

Space has weather like Earth. Solar storms occur in space.

Solar storms are explosions on the Sun's surface.

Clouds of hot gases from the explosion reach Earth's atmosphere.

They send extra **electric currents** into Earth's atmosphere.

They disrupt radio signals and GPS systems.

NATURAL DISASTERS QUIZ

1. What are made up of series of big waves?

   a) Mudslides
   b) Tsunamis
   c) Avalanches

2. Where do tornadoes come from?

   a) Floods
   b) Thunderstorms
   c) Solar storms

3. What do hurricanes form above?

   a) Warm water
   b) Icy Water
   c) Flooded rivers

4. What is a pandemic?

   a) An outbreak of disease in a neighborhood
   b) A cure to a disease
   c) An outbreak of disease across a wide area

5. What are explosions on the Sun's surface called?

   a) Solar Storms
   b) Hot Thunderstorms
   c) Star Storms

6. What becomes more likely during droughts?

   a) Floods
   b) Thunder
   c) Wildfires

Answers: 1) b 2) b 3) a 4) c 5) a 6) c

GLOSSARY

Atmosphere: the mass of gases surrounding a planet or moon

Electric currents: the flows of electricity

Epicenters: points on the Earth's surface at the center of earthquakes

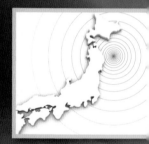

Mantle: the layer of Earth between the crust and the core

Tectonic plate: a massive, irregularly shaped slab of rock that divides the Earth's crust and on which the continents move

Outer Space

Ruth Strother

Contents

Endless Space

Outer space is huge.
The universe contains everything
we can see.
No one knows where it ends.
Stars, planets, and moons can be
found in outer space.

Stars

Stars are bright balls of burning gas.
Stars can burn for billions of years.
The Sun is a star.
It is the closest star to Earth.

People draw pretend lines between some stars.
The lines form shapes.
The shapes look like people and animals.
These shapes are called **constellations**.

The Solar System

The Sun is the only star in our solar system.
The Sun is the center of our solar system.
The word *solar* means "of the Sun."

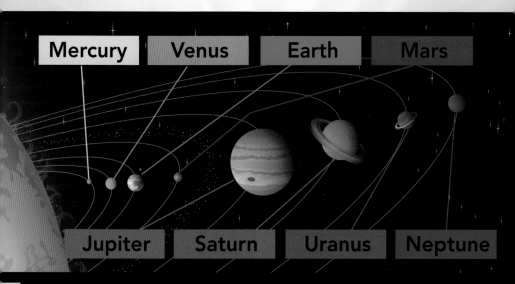

Mercury | Venus | Earth | Mars

Jupiter | Saturn | Uranus | Neptune

The Sun's **gravity** pulls planets into a path. The path leads planets around the Sun.

We live on the planet Earth.
Earth is part of the solar system.

Planets are objects in space.
Planets must follow a path around
a star.
Our solar system has eight planets.

Each planet is round.
Each planet follows a path around the Sun.
This path is called an **orbit**.
And each planet is the only big object in its orbit.

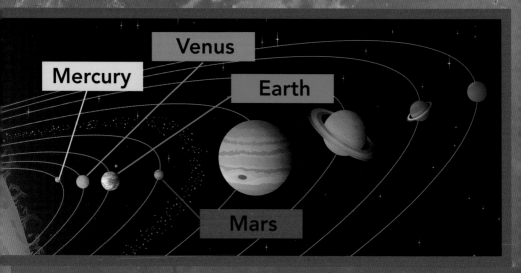

Four planets are closer to the Sun.
They are Mercury, Venus, Earth, and Mars.
They are the inner planets.

Inner planets are small, solid, and rocky.

Mercury is the smallest planet in the solar system.

Venus is the brightest planet seen from Earth.

Mercury

Venus

Earth

Mars

Earth is the only planet with liquid water on its surface.

Mars has the tallest mountain in the solar system.

Gas Planets

Saturn

Neptune

Jupiter

Uranus

The gas planets are Jupiter, Saturn, Uranus, and Neptune. They are not solid. They are gassy, almost like clouds. Spaceships can't land on them.

Jupiter is the biggest planet in the solar system.

Saturn has rings made of ice, dust, and rocks.

Uranus is the coldest planet in the solar system.

Neptune is the windiest planet in the solar system.

Jupiter

Saturn

Uranus

Neptune

Moons are space objects.
Moons orbit a planet.
The planet's gravity keeps a moon on its path.

Some planets have many moons.
Some planets have no moon at all.

Earth has one moon.

Jupiter has more moons than any other planet.
Jupiter has sixty-seven moons!

Comets

Comets are dust and rocks trapped in ice.
Comets orbit the Sun.
Comets have a tail.
The tail points away from the Sun.

Comets melt a little when they get close to the Sun.
Some comets crash into a planet or a moon.
These comets leave big holes called **craters**.

Asteroids are made of rocks.
Asteroids orbit the Sun, just like planets do.
But asteroids are too small to be planets.
Most asteroids are found between Mars and Jupiter.

Meteoroids are made of rocks and metals.
Meteoroids are smaller than asteroids.
But meteoroids orbit the Sun too.
Sometimes asteroids and meteoroids fall to Earth.

Meteors are meteoroids that get close to Earth.
Meteors burn when they get close to Earth.
Meteors look like flashes of light. We call them shooting stars!

Sometimes meteors don't burn up. Sometimes meteors land on Earth. Then they are called meteorites.

Galaxies

Galaxies are made of dust, gas, and billions of stars.
Billions of galaxies spin in outer space.
Earth and our solar system are part of a galaxy.

Our galaxy has hundreds of billions of stars!
From Earth, the stars look like a pathway of milk.
Our galaxy is called the Milky Way.

Astronauts travel to outer space. Some astronauts learn how to fly a spaceship.

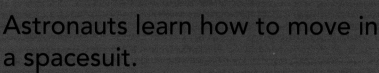

Astronauts learn how to move in a spacesuit.
Some astronauts learn how to study outer space.

astronauts

American astronauts train at NASA. But astronauts come from other countries too.

Astronauts are called cosmonauts in Russia.
The first person in space was a cosmonaut.

cosmonaut

Spaceships and Space Stations

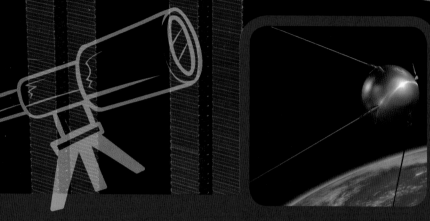

The first spaceship was the size of a soccer ball.

Now spaceships are big. Spaceships carry astronauts into outer space.

Some astronauts live and work in space.

Their job is to study outer space. They stay in outer space for many months.

These astronauts live and work in space stations.

Exploring Outer Space

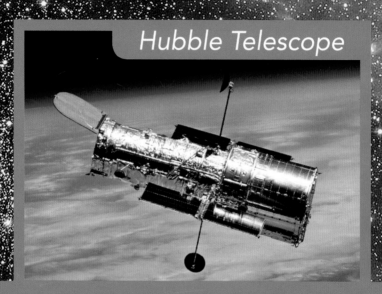

Hubble Telescope

We can't get to many parts of outer space.
So we send up robots and **telescopes**.
They explore space for us.
They send us new facts.

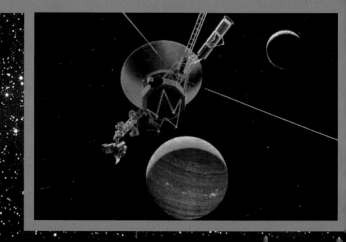

Mars Rover

We have a lot of outer space to explore.
Maybe someday you will be an astronaut.
Maybe you will work in a space station.
Maybe you will explore a new planet!

Outer Space QUIZ

1. How long can stars burn?
   a) Thousands of years
   b) Hundreds of years
   c) Billions of years

2. What does the word "solar" mean?
   a) "of outer space"
   b) "of the Sun"
   c) "of a star"

3. How many planets are in our solar system?
   a) Eight
   b) Five
   c) Nine

4. Which is the smallest planet in our solar system?
   a) Earth
   b) Jupiter
   c) Mercury

5. Which is the biggest planet in our solar system?
   a) Jupiter
   b) Saturn
   c) Mars

6. What is our galaxy called?
   a) A constellation
   b) The solar system
   c) The Milky Way

Answers: 1) c 2) b 3) a 4) c 5) a 6) c

GLOSSARY

 **constellations**: groups of stars that form shapes

craters: scooped-out areas made by space objects hitting a planet or moon

gravity: a force that pulls one object to another

 **orbit**: the path one object takes around another object

telescope: a tool that makes distant objects look closer and bigger